# Matters of Opinion

# SCHOOL VIOLENCE

BY
TONEY ALLMAN

NORWOOD HOUSE PRESS
CHICAGO, ILLINOIS

Norwood House Press
P.O. Box 316598
Chicago, Illinois 60631

For information regarding Norwood House Press, please visit our website at:
www.norwoodhousepress.com or call 866-565-2900.

PHOTO CREDITS: Cover: © Andre Babiak /Alamy; © Age Photostock/Alamy, 2; © a
katz/Shutterstock.com; 10; © Alexander Raths/Shutterstock.com, 43; © Antoniodiaz/
Dreamstime.com, 32; © Bambi L. Dingman/Dreamstime.com, 23; © Boston Globe/
Getty Images, 12; Courtesy of the Centers for Disease Control and Prevention, 9;
© Don Tremaine/Alamy, 36; © dotschock/Shutterstock.com, 41; © Fer Gregory/
Shutterstock.com, 20; © Homeriscool/Dreamstime.com, 16; © Marmaduke St. John/
Alamy, 44; © PjPhoto69/iStock Photos, 47; © Santa Monica Police Department via
Getty Images, 11; © skynesher/iStock Photos, 42; © Shutterstock.com, 7, 18; © Tim
Boyle/Getty Images, 31; © Wonderland Stock/Alamy, 35

Paperback ISBN: 978-1-60357-860-8

The Library of Congress has cataloged the original hardcover edition with the following
call number: 2015027487

290N—062016
Printed in ShenZhen, Guangdong, China.

# Contents

Note: Words that are **bolded** in the text are defined in the glossary.

# Timeline

**1764** The first school shooting in the United States occurs when four Lenape Native Americans entered a schoolhouse and killed a teacher and, while reports varied about the numbers, at least nine children.

**1866** An editorial in the *New York Times* condemns the common student practice of carrying pistols to school.

**1890s** Most reported school violence by students involves stabbings with knives and hitting with stones.

**1903** In South Carolina, 17-year-old student Edward Foster attempts to stop his male teacher from whipping him by jerking away the teacher's rod. The rod hits the pistol the teacher holds in self-defense and the pistol fires, killing Foster.

**1927** "Maniac bomber" Andrew Kehoe, a school board member, plants a series of bombs under a Bath, Michigan, school, killing 38 children and seven adults.

**1974** In Olean, New York, 17-year-old Anthony Barbaro uses a rifle and shotgun to kill three people and wound eleven at his high school.

**1982** Joe Clark becomes principal of East Side High School in Patterson, New Jersey. Determined to stop the violence in the school, he expels 300 students in one day for fighting, abusing teachers, and vandalism. (The 1989 film "Lean on Me" celebrates Clark's discipline style at the school.)

**1992** The American Medical Association labels youth violence as a public health issue.

**1994** The US Congress passes a "zero tolerance" law requiring all public schools to expel any student who carries a gun to school.

**1997** · In Paducah, Kentucky, 14-year-old Michael Carneal opens fire on fellow students, killing three and wounding five more.

**1998** · Two middle school boys, aged 13 and 11, take seven guns to school in Jonesboro, Arkansas, pull a fire alarm, and shoot people as they exit the school. Four students and one teacher are killed; nine others are wounded.

**1999** · At Columbine High School in Colorado, Dylan Klebold and Eric Harris kill 12 students and one teacher before turning their guns on themselves.

**2008** · The American Psychological Association says that zero tolerance policies as schools currently apply them have failed to achieve fair discipline and safe schools.

**2009** · Florida passes a law stopping schools from reporting minor violence (such as fighting) or minor theft to police and urges schools to seek alternatives to long-term suspensions or expulsions.

**2011** · Texas A&M University releases a report claiming that punishments are used unevenly across races, abilities, and schools. The unfairness harms students, often leading to dropping out of school or failing a grade.

**2012** · A gunman enters Sandy Hook Elementary school in Newtown, Connecticut, and opens fire, killing 20 first graders and six school staff. It is the deadliest school shooting in American history.

**2014** · Jaylen Fryberg, aged 15, shoots fellow students at Marsyville-Pilchuck High School in Seattle, Washington, then kills himself. Four of his five victims also die.

# 1 The Problem of School Violence

First Lady Michelle Obama says that violence in school is a big concern. Students from one high school in Chicago told her that they were scared at school. Obama says that "every day they wake up and wonder whether they're going to make it out of school alive."[1] The kids at this high school worry about the dangers of guns and other weapons in school. They worry about gangs attacking people at school. They worry about fights or getting beaten up. Millions of kids attend schools where violence is a problem every day.

Most kids go to schools where they feel safe. These students do not fear daily violence. But even those students can have trouble. In 2014 researchers at the University of New Hampshire asked students about violent acts in their schools. The students ranged from 5 years old to 17 years old. Fourteen percent said that they had been victims of some kind of violence at school. Six percent stayed home from school at least one day because they

*Bullying is a form of school violence.*

were scared of violence. The researchers say, "Too many kids are missing school because they do not feel safe."[2]

# What Is School Violence?

The US Centers for Disease Control and Prevention (CDC) keeps track of school violence. It says school violence is a public health issue and affects the well-being of young people. The CDC keeps track of all the facts about what school violence means and how it hurts students.

The CDC says that school violence can take many forms. All these forms are types of **aggression**. Using weapons is one kind of school violence. Violence can also mean fighting, punching, kicking, hitting, or slapping. Bullying is another kind of school violence. Aggression and threats over the Internet can be a form of violence, too.

# How Common Is School Violence?

Weapon use can lead to the worst kind of school violence. In 2013 the CDC said that 7.7 percent of high school students were threatened or injured with a weapon on school grounds. About 16 percent of high school students have carried a gun to school. The CDC reports that between 14 and 34 school-aged kids are killed in school violence incidents every year. But the use of weapons is only one kind of school violence. In 2011, for instance, 597,500 students were injured in acts of school violence. That is about 1 percent of students in school. Some of them were hurt by weapons, but some were injured in fights. In 2010, 74 percent of all public schools reported at least one case of violent crime in the past year.

Any amount of violence at school worries people. The US Department of Justice says, "Our nation's schools should be **safe havens** for teaching and learning, free of crime and violence."[3] Fifty million kids are enrolled in schools in the United States. That is a lot of people at risk for violence and aggression. Experts worry about why violence occurs at school at all. They want to know what can be done to decrease the risk and keep schools safe.

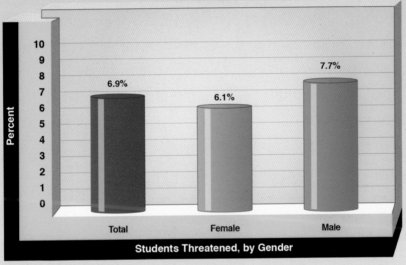

**Percentage of High School Students Threatened or Injured with a Weapon\*
on School Property,\*\* Centers for Disease Control and Prevention,
Youth Risk Behavior Surveillance System (YRBSS) 2013**

\* For example, a gun, knife, or club

\*\* One or more times during the 12 months before the survey

Taken from: National Youth Risk Behavior Survey Overview. www.cdc.gov.

# No Easy Answers

Why does school violence happen? What can be done
to stop it? There are no easy answers to these questions.
Experts worry about why violence happens and how to
change that behavior.

# Violence and Gun Control

The number of murders with guns in the United States was 19.5 times more than in all other countries in 2011, according to the United Nations. In the United States, guns are common, and gun control is not very strict. In other wealthy countries, guns can be hard to get. In 1996, for instance, Australia passed strict gun control laws. The laws made it very difficult to own a gun. Gun deaths were cut in half in that country. Some people believe strict gun control would stop much school violence.

The United States' high murder rate causes many people to call for stricter gun control laws.

*A suspected mass shooting gunman is shown entering the Santa Monica College library during his rampage on June 7, 2013.*

Parents and students want answers about school violence, too. A third of parents are afraid their children are not safe from violence at school. About 10 percent of kids say that they worry about being safe at school. Hector Villalba, for example, is 16 years old. He attends a high school in Arizona and worries about crime, fights, and guns at his school. He says, "Someone could come in with a sports bag that's big enough to carry an assault rifle or something, and no one would notice. I cannot live in fear. I cannot be held hostage to the idea that it could happen."[4]

In one poll taken in 2014, parents ranked school violence and shootings among their top ten fears about their kids. Many teachers also fear violence at school. They fear for their own safety. They worry about how to protect their students from violent acts. Baltimore teacher Jeff Slattery was assaulted by a student in the hall of his high school. The student beat Slattery and broke his jaw. One study found that 7 percent of teachers cope with threats or assaults each year. Reporter Scottie Hughes says that when teachers are not safe, kids cannot feel safe either. She says, "When the authority figures in our

Teacher Colleen Ritzer was killed by a student at Danvers High School in October 2013. Teachers are also targeted during teen shooting sprees.

## Teen Dating Violence

One of the causes of school violence is dating violence. Girls are more likely to suffer serious injury than boys. Some victims are severely abused. Some teens are raped on school grounds. This happened to a girl in Texas. She was raped in an empty band room. Some are killed by their dating partners. In 1997, Luke Woodham went to school and shot his ex-girlfriend and a friend who was with her. Dating violence, in or out of school, is a serious problem for young people.

schools are abused and threatened . . . , kids do not feel protected and lose their focus and their respect for the system that cannot even protect the adults."[5]

## A Look Inside This Book

School violence is a difficult problem to solve. Many different kinds of school violence exist. No one has easy solutions. People have different ideas about what causes it, what can be done about it, and how to prevent it.

In this book, three issues are discussed in more detail: Does a violent culture cause school violence? Is school security the answer to the school violence problem? Can schools teach non-violence? Each chapter ends with a section called **Examine the Opinions**, which highlights one argumentation technique used in the chapter. At the end of the book, students can test their skills at writing their own essay based on the book's topic. Notes, glossary, a bibliography, and an index in the back provide additional resources.

# 2 Does a Violent Culture Cause School Violence?

 **Yes:** The Culture Is To Blame for School Violence

College professor Henry A. Giroux studies culture in the United States and Canada. He claims that our culture is soaked in violence. Society is addicted to violence and even war. The United States has been involved in several wars. Young people are trained to be soldiers. But it is not just soldiers who use guns. During wartime, people begin to think of violence as the norm. The police use force to control people. That is a kind of violence, too. More than 47 percent of Americans own guns. Guns kill at least 84 people every day. Strict gun control laws do not exist, so almost anyone can own a gun. It is easy for people to get and use weapons. But Giroux says that the issue of violence in society is bigger than guns. He argues, "The issue of violence in

America goes far beyond the issue of gun control."[6] Popular culture embraces violence at every level. People like and accept violence. They watch it and practice it all the time. Sports are violent. Movies are violent. TV news is filled with violence. People love to play violent video games. Violence is a way of life.

Giroux explains, "There is no one cause of violence." He says it is caused by the war on drugs, from police

*Popular culture embraces violence at every level.*

# Desensitized to Violence

"Desensitized" to violence means numb to it or not bothered by it. Experts say that this can happen to anyone. Students at Rutgers University wrote an editorial in their newspaper. It was about what causes violence. They think that kids are desensitized to it because of movies and TV. The students wrote, "As a nation, Americans have become desensitized to the idea of violence. There are children's movies and television shows that involve harmless kicking and punching, but as children grow older the need for stimulation begins to [increase]. . . . Seeing such acts of violence on a daily basis . . . blurs the line between fiction and reality creating a culture around attack and assault as the answer."

*Daily Targum* (Rutgers University), "Desensitization Leads to School Shootings: Culture Surrounding School Shootings Is Overly Relaxed," February 17, 2015. www.dailytargum.com.

acting like soldiers in war, and from too many people going to prison. It comes from soldiers trained to be killers. The result is "a dangerous culture of violence and cruelty."[7]

# Learning Violence from the Media

Many people agree that Americans live in a violent culture. Typical American kids see a lot of violence on television. They view 16,000 murders on TV by the time they are 18 years old. They view 200,000 other acts of violence. Many doctors say that watching so much violence harms kids. They get numb to violence. They are so used to it that it does not bother or upset them in real life. They think violence is normal and feel no pity or

*Kids join gangs because a violent lifestyle seems normal to them.*

sympathy for victims. They may feel that violence is the right way to settle arguments. Dr. Eugene V. Beresin says, "Heroes are violent, and, as such, are rewarded for their behavior. They become role models for youth. It is 'cool' to carry an automatic weapon and use it to knock off the 'bad guys.'" Then, Beresin says, kids come to see violence as "a fact of life."[8] They may imitate violent acts in their own lives. They may use violence to get back at a bully. They may use violence to solve problems at school.

## But Not So Fast...

**No:** The Culture Is Not To Blame for School Violence

Is American culture really so violent? Psychologist Steven Pinker says it is not. He says violence in the world has declined. He explains that the world used to be much more violent than it is today. In the Middle Ages, for example, the murder rate was 35 times the murder rate today. In the modern world, most countries are at peace with each other. Pinker says reason and learning "have led people to

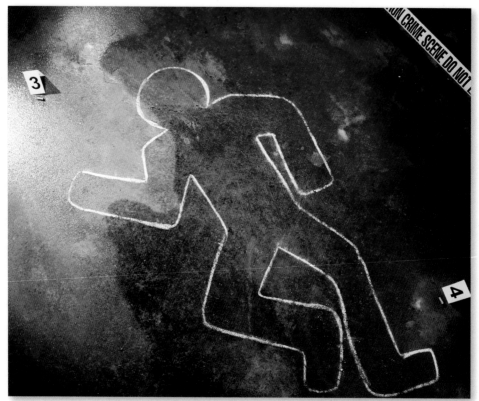

*Though many people think the murder rate has increased, it has actually continued to decrease.*

think of violence as a problem to be solved rather than as a contest to be won."[9]

Crime is a problem, but it is no worse than it used to be; in fact, it is much better. The FBI reports that violent crimes have fallen since 1993 and murders are down by 50 percent. Society is not more violent today; it is less violent. The public is not unsafe. People are just more aware of violent crimes because they are reported so much in the media. Even in schools where gangs are common, most kids are not members of gangs. Pinker says that violence is one part of the human mind. He says, "Violence committed by a small number of individuals is

## Maybe It Is the School, Not the Culture

Something as simple as the size of a school may cause violence and aggression. Many studies show that violence is more common in large schools than in small ones. This is true no matter where the schools are. David A. Kaiser studies human brains. He says that human brains do not cope well in large schools. The schools are too complex. Students feel isolated and confused. They have a hard time fitting in. Kaiser says every high school should be limited to 600 students. That is about 150 kids in each grade. Kaiser says that is "the natural group size of humans." Yet many schools today have more than 1,000 students. Kaiser argues, "When more than half of all public high schools exceed our natural group size, it is not surprising that abnormal and atypical social behaviors including violence frequently occur." A violent culture is not the problem. The problem is a society that builds large schools.

David A. Kaiser, "School Shootings, High School Size, and Neurobiological Considerations," Haworth Press, 2005. www.skiltopo.com.

unlikely to go away."[10] This small number of people may cause the violence in society and in school. But the culture as a whole is not violent.

# School Violence and Personal Responsibility

Years ago, two male teens shot and killed thirteen fellow students at Columbine High School in Colorado. They wounded twenty-three more students. Then the two teens killed themselves. Many people blamed America's culture of violence. They blamed society's gun culture. They blamed violent media. Dr. Timothy Wheeler rejects those ideas. He says the culture is not to blame. Wheeler explains, "Generations of Americans have grown up around guns without feeling at all compelled to commit multiple murders. . . . If guns themselves don't cause criminal behavior, another popular explanation is the long-term effects of violent television, movies, and video games. . . . In fact, only a fraction of the millions of children exposed to TV violence go on to imitate the **mayhem** they have seen portrayed on the screen. These explanations fail because

*After the Columbine High School shootings in 1999, many people blamed America's culture of violence.*

they try to pin the blame for violence on something outside the individual—they deny that these young men are ultimately responsible for their own actions."[11]

School violence is caused by individuals with serious problems. Mental health experts describe some of the factors that may make kids violent. Sometimes violent people are mentally or emotionally sick. The violence is a part of the sickness. This is not society's fault. It is the student and the family who are troubled. Perhaps society needs to improve its mental health system. Maybe troubled people do not get enough help and counseling. But a violent culture is not the problem. The problem is hate-filled people who choose to commit violent acts at school.

# Closing Arguments

Whether a violent culture causes school violence is an issue. Some people believe the culture is terribly violent. This teaches kids to be violent. Others argue that society is less violent than at any time in history. School violence is caused by a few disturbed individuals who choose to be aggressive. Whether violence is an issue of personal responsibility or the fault of society continues to be a matter of debate.

# Examine the Opinions

## Bias

In this chapter, the two opposing essays have a bias about the causes of school violence. A bias is a strong opinion about something. That opinion can be positive or negative. In the first essay, the author has a negative bias about American culture. She believes the culture is violent and therefore causes school violence. She presents only the facts that support that belief. In the second half of the chapter, the author argues that the culture today is not to blame for school violence. She says the culture is not violent. School violence is a matter of personal responsibility. These opinions are supported by arguments supporting those points of view. Everyone has biases. None of the arguments are wrong. But each is supported by a different set of facts and a different way of thinking about the world. A reader might not agree with any of the opinions, and that is okay. But be aware of the biases and think about them. Are they supported by facts? Are facts omitted? Are the biases fair? Try to recognize biases when you come across them, and then form your own opinion.

# 3 Is School Security the Answer to the School Violence Problem?

## 👍 Yes: The Number One Priority for All Schools Is To Keep Students Safe

Many people do not care why school violence happens. They just want to guard against it and keep schools safe. Some schools take extreme security measures to solve the problem of violence. Middleton Elementary School is one of those schools. It is just outside Chicago. At this school, no one can enter school grounds without being checked out. Barricades line the school's entrance and parking lot. Cars are not allowed too close to the school's front door. People have to ring the school's doorbell to get inside. Windows are all around the front door. The doorbell has a video camera. School staff can look at the visitor through the windows and on

*Some schools take extra security measures to solve the problem of violence, such as issuing school IDs.*

the camera. They check to see whether the person looks safe. Only then is the visitor let in the first door, where a staff member waits. The visitor has to show an ID card, and the school runs a **background check** right away. If the visitor passes the check, he or she receives a photo ID to wear inside the school. Even parents have to wear one.

Teachers and kids at Middleton like all of this security. They are not afraid that a shooter could get into their school. Teacher Dara Sacher says, "I think the most important thing is just keeping the kids safe." Parents are happy with the strict security, too. One parent, Charlene Abraham, says, "We're sending our kids to school to learn, not to worry about whether they're going to come home or not."[12]

# Normal School Safety Procedures

Middleton is a high-security school. Most schools cannot afford such strict security measures. But the US Department of Education reports that most schools have safety procedures in place. For public schools, 88 percent keep the buildings locked or guard the doors during school hours. Security cameras operate in 64 percent of schools. In about 42 percent of schools, armed security officers patrol the hallways. Other schools use metal detectors to check students as they enter the building. Some check book bags and backpacks as kids enter the school. Others ban backpacks and book bags for safety reasons. All of these measures keep schools safe. No

## No Amount of Security Is Too Much

In a few schools, teachers decide to carry guns to protect their students. In seven states, laws allow teachers to carry concealed weapons to school. Kasey Hansen is a teacher in Salt Lake City, Utah. She carries a handgun to the classroom every day. She says, "I want to protect my students. I'm going to stand in front of a bullet for any student that is in my protection and so I want another option to defend us." A student in school might become a rampage shooter. An outsider might come into the school to attack kids. Hansen wants to be ready to fight back. Armed teachers are one more layer of security that can protect kids from school violence.

Quoted in Kate Murphy, "'F' Is for Firearm: More Teachers Authorized to Carry Weapons in Classroom," News21, NBC News, September 22, 2014, www.nbcnews.com.

one can enter the school that does not belong there. No one can carry weapons into the school.

## Zero Tolerance Policies

Armed guards and secured buildings keep schools safe. Punishing bad behavior at school keeps schools safer, too. About 75 percent of public schools have **zero tolerance** policies to control student actions at school. A zero tolerance policy means that breaking any school rule is strictly punished. There are no exceptions to the policy. There are no excuses. The school does not allow any bad behavior. Zero tolerance policies clearly tell kids what actions are not okay. The punishment is so harsh that kids are scared to break the rules. Zero tolerance helps keep schools safe from violence.

## But Not So Fast...

 **No:** **Extreme Security Does Not Prevent Violence**

In 2013 the National Association of School Psychologists (NASP) put out a report that looked at types of school security. The NASP report does not support extreme security measures. It says, "There is no clear evidence that the use of metal detectors, security cameras, or guards in schools are effective in preventing school violence. In fact, evidence suggests that students

*Schools use metal detectors to search students as part of zero tolerance policies.*

believe their schools to be safe places and that their schools' security strategies are unnecessary."[13]

Also, NASP says that strict discipline is not a good security measure. It does more harm than good. Many experts agree with this idea. Zero tolerance policies may hurt kids and do not really work. Asher Palmer was expelled from his school in 2014 for pretending to shoot classmates with a toy gun. Asher's "gun" was a tube made out of rolled-up paper. Asher also got in a fight

*Kids who bring toy guns to school are being expelled as part of zero tolerance policies.*

with a girl in his class. He told her he wanted to kill her. Asher is eight years old and has **ADHD**. His school is for kids with special needs. The school principal said that Asher is "physically and verbally aggressive."[14] She says Asher is a risk to other students. Is it common sense to punish a little boy like this for playing? Is Asher really a danger to his school? Is he violent? Common sense answers "No" to these questions. Zero tolerance policies go too far when a child like Asher is expelled.

# Zero Tolerance or Zero Justice?

Many times, zero tolerance policies lead to harsh and unjust punishment. Atiya Haynes was expelled from her school because of a pocket knife. Atiya is 17 years old and lives in a dangerous area of Detroit. Her grandfather

## Schools Are Not Supposed to Be Like Jails

In 2013, Mike Ruff was a senior at H.D. Woodson High School in Washington, DC. The school is an inner-city school. Many of the kids are minority students. Ruff and other students hated the security in their school. They said their school felt like a prison. Ruff had to take off his belt every day to go through the metal detector. He said it was "like you're going to visit somebody" in jail. He did not like the high fence around the school either. It looked like an ugly prison fence. Ruff said, "Why is it even there? It serves no purpose." Ruff explained, "We want our school to be more like a school. Other schools don't have police officers. So why does our school have to have that?"

Quoted in Annie Gowen, "D.C. Students Use Photography to Protest School Security," *Washington Post*, April 4, 2013, www.washingtonpost.com.

was worried about her, so he gave her a small pocket knife for protection. Atiya put the knife in her purse and forgot about it when she went to school. During a bag search, school staff found the knife. It did not matter that Atiya forgot about the knife. The school said she was carrying a dangerous weapon. Atiya tried to convince the school that it was an accident. She just made a mistake. Atiya said, "I'm not a bad kid at all. I've seen so many statistics in my life of what not to be and I try so hard not to go down that path and for something like this to affect what I'm trying to be. . . . And this is an issue that is not just affecting me; it's something that's nationwide. No-tolerance policies are . . . unjust. It doesn't give a chance to explain or acknowledge circumstances."[15]

Atiya is a minority student. Many people say that zero tolerance hurts minority students the most. That is why the American Bar Association (ABA) does not like zero tolerance policies. The US Department of Justice reports that African American kids are three times more likely to be expelled or suspended than Caucasian kids. These kids are not violent people. But they are treated like they are. Jody Owens II is a lawyer who fights for

*Many people say that zero tolerance hurts minority students the most.*

racial justice. He says, "The unwritten policy is that African American kids are bad students. But if we look at patterns and practices, we see that African American students are disciplined at an alarming rate."[16] Minority kids, disabled kids, and poor kids are harmed by zero tolerance. The policies are just not fair to them.

*Strict security makes schools uninviting and may in turn be doing more harm than good.*

# Security Does Not Help Kids

Schools should be comfortable places where students feel welcome and want to learn. Strict security makes some schools feel like prisons. Armed guards, student searches, metal detectors, and strict rules may do more harm than good. Susan Brott is an educator who thinks security can go too far. She says, "There's a fine line between building a fortress and maintaining a safe and caring learning center."[17] Too much security tells students they are not trusted. It makes schools uninviting and it sends the wrong message to kids.

# Closing Arguments

Whether strict security keeps schools safe from violence is debatable. Many people feel safe with armed guards, locked doors, student searches, and other measures. Many hope that zero tolerance policies will prevent any kind of student violence. Others object to so much security. They worry that schools feel more and more like jails. They point out that zero tolerance policies hurt kids who do not deserve it. The kind of security that works best for schools and kids is still an issue.

# Examine the Opinions

## Evaluating Sources of Information

In this book, the author uses a variety of sources that are cited in the back of the book under the Notes section. When writing an essay, quoting from and citing sources shows a reader that you have done your research. The reader can not only glance through this essay to get an idea of what types of sources you've used, but also to possibly verify some of the sources and use them as part of their own research.

While citing your research can make your piece more credible, not all sources are equal in value. Some sources can be very relevant and useful to a topic, while others may not be. For example, a reader should examine a writer's sources for bias, authority, and relevance to the topic. One way to evaluate a writer's sources is to see how old the material is that is quoted. An older source may be quickly outdated on a current topic such as a disease or immigration law. But an older source may be reliable if it was a landmark study or a historically significant piece.

A reader should also pay special attention to online sources. Some online sources are merely digital versions of print sources, such as newspapers. Magazines and newspapers go through a review and editing process and are usually credible sources. Websites are other sources that deserve more investigation. Is the website's creator a reliable source? How long has the website been established? Does it have a clear bias or point of view that it is promoting?

Take a look at the Notes section to glance through the sources the author used to compile this chapter on school safety. The author used a lot of testimonials from people who have strong opinions. It is important to note that the people quoted were not quoting research, but only giving their own opinion based on their personal and professional experience.

The author used a variety of online sources. Some of these online sources were digital versions of print sources, such as *The Washington Post* newspaper. She also used material from major TV news sources, such as abcnews.com. Using the criteria established above, do you think the author used good sources for this chapter?

# 4 Can Schools Teach Non-violence?

**Yes:** Educational Programs Can Reduce the Risk of Violence in Schools

Schools can change the social climate for the better with lessons that teach students non-violence. Every student in the school takes part in these lessons. The lessons are called "**universal violence prevention programs**." In the classroom, students learn social skills for solving problems in a peaceful way. They learn to get along with their peers. They learn to understand violence and why it happens. All these activities reduce the risk of violence at school.

## A Good Behavior Program

One program for younger kids is called PAX Good Behavior Game. *Pax* means "peace" in Latin. In this program, the class is divided into three teams. They stay

*Good behavior games like PAX are designed to help students cooperate with one another.*

in these teams during the school day. The teams compete to earn small rewards for good behavior. They have to try to pay attention, not disrupt the group, and avoid aggressive behavior. The program sounds simple, but it seems to benefit kids in the long run. Studies show that kids who played the game do better throughout their school lives. By the time they are grown, the students who played the game stay out of trouble more than the kids who did not play the game. Fewer get suspended or act violently in school. Fewer become delinquents or go to jail. Fewer abuse alcohol or drugs. Researchers say that young kids can learn to be peaceful and cooperative. They learn **social skills**. Then, these lessons help the kids avoid violence as they grow up.

# An Anti-bullying Program

Programs for older kids include anti-bullying programs. The idea is that stopping bullying at school stops all kinds

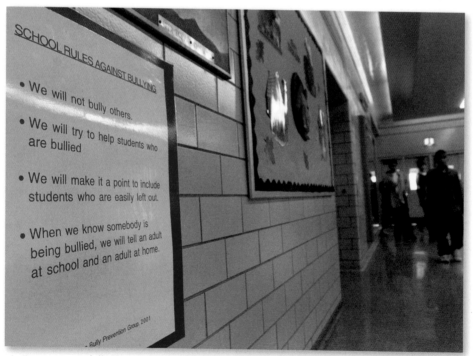

*A Denver middle school institutes the Olweus bullying prevention program. Such programs have significantly reduced bullying incidents in school.*

As in Norway, some schools in the United States have prevention programs that offer counseling and group meetings for kids whose tests indicate they may commit violent acts.

of violence. Dan Olweus, a psychologist in Norway, developed one such bullying prevention program. It is used in schools around the world. Everyone in the school participates. Teachers and school staff learn to recognize bullying. They set up rules against bullying. They promise to stop bullying whenever they see it. They learn to praise and reward any kid who reports bullying. Students learn what bullying is, too. They have regular group meetings to talk about bullying and how to prevent

# Prevention Programs Change Behavior

In 2014 Dr. Manny Sethi and his research team did a study in a middle school in Nashville, Tennessee. The school had a lot of problems with violence. The team ran a prevention program for 122 kids in the school. The kids learned about peaceful ways to get along. They learned how to deal with violence. Sethi says, "This is about giving our children the tools they need. . . . This program is about developing the mental machinery to deal with conflict in a peaceful way. What we need to do as a community is come together and combat these things. If we rely on the power of our communities across Tennessee we can do amazing things."

Quoted in Vanderbilt University Medical Center Newsroom, "School Violence Intervention Program Effective in Vanderbilt Pilot Study," Newswise.com, April 11, 2014.

it. They have fun activities like acting out what to do or say if they see bullying. They learn to argue with words instead of being violent. They tell a teacher if they see anyone being a bully in the school. They draw posters and produce videos about bullying. Researchers say that the program reduces violence, vandalism, fighting, and skipping school. It reduces reports of bullying in the school. Kids in schools with the program even get better grades. One school principal says, "The *Olweus Bullying Prevention Program* has had a positive impact on our entire school of over 650 students and staff. . . . [In one year] the reported bullying referrals have decreased by 68 percent."[18]

## But Not So Fast...

 **No: Prevention Programs Are Not the Whole Answer to School Violence**

Universal violence prevention programs do not always work. Targeted prevention programs have problems, too. Ronald W. Pies is a psychiatrist who studies violence in teens. He says, "There are no simple answers or easy remedies."[19] Sometimes, social problems are the cause of violence. Social problems like neighborhood gangs may lead to violent acts at school. Other times, emotional disorders or mental illnesses lead to violent acts. No single prevention program can address all the issues that can cause violence to erupt.

# Nothing Works All the Time

Some universal programs work well and some do not. Researchers need more evidence to know which programs are good at reducing school violence. Several universal programs have been studied. These programs do help schools reduce some kinds of violence. They reduce bullying, fighting, and aggression. They can help kids feel safe at school. But there is no evidence that they lower the risk of deadly violence. Rampage shootings are still poorly understood. Researchers do not know what makes some kids become killers. Sometimes mental illness is to blame. Sometimes it may be bullying. Sometimes it is abuse at home. Maybe the problem is when kids watch too much violent media. Maybe it happens when a person is feeling alone and friendless. No one knows for sure. Most people with these troubles never become violent. No one knows how to tell who will react with rampage violence and who will not. At

*Social problems may lead some students to act out violently at school.*

the University of Michigan, writer Shaun Dolan says, "There is no way to answer *who kills?* . . . The only real criteria for the school shooter is that they are a student and have horrific motives."[20]

Pies agrees with Dolan. Pies explains that science has no sure way to tell who may become violent. No tests can

# Teaching the Wrong Thing

Stuart Twemlow is a doctor and an expert on school violence. He wrote an important book about bullies and violence. He says that anti-bullying programs can backfire. Sometimes, bullying gets worse in schools with prevention programs. The programs tell bullies how to be better bullies. Twemlow says,

> If you have a list that says do this, this and this in the case of a bully, the thing you've got to remember is that bullies read them too. Bullies are just as intelligent as other people. Bullies are not the cause of the problem. They're the result of the problem. The problem is in the climate of the school. And when you have a lot of bullies at a school, you have a problem with the leadership of the school. And that's complicated.

Twemlow says that adults have to change. The school staff has to change. School rules and morals have to change. Schools need to be places of kindness. Targeting bad behavior with prevention programs is not enough to make that happen.

Quoted in Alexander Trowbridge, "Are Anti-bullying Efforts Making It Worse?," CBS News, October 10, 2013, www.cbsnews.com.

predict who will commit violent acts. So there is no true way to tell what needs to be taught in special programs. High risk does not mean much in real life. It can be useful some of the time, but it is not certain. Pies adds, "We will probably never be able to predict who will act violently, much less predict such rare events as mass shootings in schools. Stereotyped profiles [descriptions] aimed at such prediction do not seem useful."[21] Maybe rampage violence can never be prevented completely. Maybe no prevention program can teach shooters not to want to kill. Pies says that researchers have to keep trying to understand people who decide to kill. Society needs to look for ways to help troubled young people. Only then, will we truly be able to stop most school violence.

# Closing Arguments

Whether schools can teach non-violence is unproven. Classroom lessons that teach social skills and reduce bullying and aggression seem to work. They can reduce bullying and fighting in schools. Targeted programs that identify and offer extra help to aggressive kids may reduce school violence, too. Many of these lessons and programs seem like good ideas. But there is no proof that they work all the time. Targeted programs may be unfair to some kids. Reducing ordinary violence is one thing. Stopping deadly violence is another. It is much harder, and no one knows what works. The issue of how to prevent school shootings remains complex and confusing.

# Examine the Opinions

## Examples

An example illustrates a general idea. Examples can be events, quotes, or small stories that support your theme. Examples build up an argument and can prove a point of view. They make the idea simple and concrete. Examples are good techniques for opinion writing. In this chapter, the author uses examples to show that prevention programs work. One example is the PAX Good Behavior Game. It explains how a prevention program might work. Another example is a quote from a school principal. The quote shows how one principal feels about the Olweus Bullying Prevention Program. It illustrates an expert's experience with a successful prevention program. Examples can be used to persuade people that an argument is valid. A good essay includes at least one example as evidence to support the opinion. Try to notice the use of examples when you read. Are they good examples? Do the examples support the theme? Are they convincing? Do they fit with the main idea? A bad example does not fit with the theme. For instance, a story about a program that teaches kids how to read well is not a good fit in this chapter. It would not support the argument. Learning to read has nothing to do with violence prevention programs. Always ask yourself whether the example helps to prove the argument.

# Wrap It Up!

## Write Your Own Essay

In this book, the author gave many opinions about school violence. These opinions can be used to write a short essay on violence in schools. Short opinion essays are a common writing form. They are also a good way to use the ideas in this book. The author gave several common argumentation techniques and evidence that can be used. Evaluating sources, bias, and the use of examples were some techniques used in the essays to sway the reader. Any of these could be used in a piece of writing.

There are 6 steps to follow when writing an essay:

## Step One: Choose a Topic

When writing your essay, first choose a topic. You can start with one of the three chapter questions from the table of contents in this book.

## Step Two: Choose Your Theme

Decide which side of the issue you will take. After choosing your topic, use the materials in this book to write the thesis, or theme, of your essay. You can use the titles of the articles in this book or the sidebar titles as examples of themes. The first paragraph should state your theme. In an essay titled "Good Security Can Prevent School Violence," state your opinion. Say why you think school security protects students from violence. You could also use a short anecdote, or story, that proves your point and will interest your reader.

## Step Three: Research Your Topic

You will need to do some further research to find enough material for your topic. You can find useful books and articles to look up in the bibliography and the notes of this book. Be sure to cite your sources, using the notes at the back of this book as an example.

## Step Four: The Body of the Essay

In the next three paragraphs, develop this theme. To develop your essay, come up with three reasons why school security works. For example, three reasons could be:

- *Building security measures keep out dangerous people.*
- *Student searches stop any weapons from entering the school.*
- *Zero tolerance policies force kids to follow rules that ban any objects that could cause harm.*

These three ideas should each be given their own paragraph. Be sure to give a piece of evidence in each paragraph. This could be a researcher's report of the number of violent acts that occur in schools every year. It could include a survey of whether students feel safe having metal detectors in their school. Each paragraph should end with a transition sentence that sums up the main idea in the paragraph and moves the reader to the next one.

## Step Five: Write the Conclusion

The final, or fifth, paragraph should state your conclusion. This should restate your theme and sum up the ideas in your essay. It could also end with an engaging quote or piece of evidence that wraps up your essay.

## Step Six: Review Your Work

Finally, be sure to reread your essay. Does it have quotes, facts, and/or anecdotes to support your conclusions? Are your ideas clearly presented? Have another reader take a look at it to see if someone else can understand your ideas. Make any changes that you think can help make your essay better.

Congratulations on using the ideas in this book to write a personal essay!

# Notes

## Chapter 1: The Problem of School Violence

1. Quoted in Justin Sink, "Michelle Obama: Gun Violence Has Children Fearing Death Every Day," *The Hill*, May 3, 2013. http://thehill.com.

2. University of New Hampshire. "Research Highlights Extent, Effects of School Violence in U.S." ScienceDaily, October 21, 2014. www.sciencedaily.com.

3. National Center for Education Statistics, Bureau of Justice Statistics, "Indicators of School Crime and Safety: 2012," June, 2013, p. 2. http://nces.ed.gov/pubs2013.

4. Quoted in BrieAnna Frank, "Valley Teachers Don't Fear Safety Despite School Violence Increase," Spot 127 Media Center, Rio Salado College. http://spot127.org/.

5. Scottie Hughes, "Why Is Violence Against Teachers Being Covered Up?," Townhall.com, October 7, 2013. http://townhall.com.

## Chapter 2: Does a Violent Culture Cause School Violence?

6. Henry A. Giroux, Interview with C.J. Polychroniou, "Violence Is Deeply Rooted in American Culture: An Interview with Henry A. Giroux," Truth-Out.org, January 17, 2013. http://truth-out.org.

7. Henry A. Giroux, Interview with C.J. Polychroniou, "Violence Is Deeply Rooted in American Culture: An Interview with Henry A. Giroux."

8. Eugene V. Beresin, "The Impact of Media Violence on Children and Adolescents: Opportunities for Clinical Interventions," DevelopMentor, American Academy of Child & Adolescent Psychiatry, 2014. www.aacap.org.

9. Steven Pinker, Interview with Ayesha Venkataraman, "Why America Is More Violent than Other Democracies," *U.S. News & World Report*, December 23, 2011. www.usnews.com.

10. Steven Pinker, Interview with Ayesha Venkataraman, "Why America Is More Violent than Other Democracies."

11. Timothy Wheeler, "Blaming the Guns, Again," The Claremont Institute, 1999. www.leaderu.com.

## Chapter 3: Is School Security the Answer to the School Violence Problem?

12. Quoted in Alex Perez and Matthew Jaffe, "School Safety: Inside One School's Extraordinary Security Measures," ABC News, December 19, 2012. http://abcnews.go.com/.

13. National Association of School Psychologists, "Research on School Security: The Impact of Security Measures on Students," NASP Online, 2013. www.nasponline.org.

14. Quoted in Carl Campanile, "Toy Gun Made of Paper Gets Kid Tossed from School," New York Post, June 16, 2014. http://nypost.com.

15. Quoted in Allie Gross, "The Zero-Tolerance Trap," Slate, October 13, 2014. www.slate.com.

16. Quoted in Stephanie Francis Ward, "Schools Start to Rethink Zero Tolerance Policies," ABA Journal, August 1, 2014. www.abajournal.com.

17. Quoted in Paul Levy, "As Minnesota Schools Enhance Security, How Much Is Too Much?," Star Tribune (Minneapolis/St. Paul), September 2, 2013. www.startribune.com.

## Chapter 4: Can Schools Teach Non-Violence?

18. Quoted in "Endorsements for the Olweus Bullying Prevention Program," Violence Prevention Works! Hazelden Foundation, 2014. www.violencepreventionworks.org.

19. Ronald W. Pies, "Before the Bullets Fly, Can We Intervene with Troubled Adolescents?," Medscape Psychiatry, January 8, 2013, p. 1. www.medscape.com.

20. Shaun Dolan, "Who's a School Shooter?" School Violence, UM Site Maker, University of Michigan. http://sitemaker.umich.edu

21. Pies, "Before the Bullets Fly, Can We Intervene with Troubled Adolescents?," p. 5.

# Glossary

**ADHD**: Short for attention-deficit/hyperactivity disorder; a disorder characterized by being overactive, unable to focus on schoolwork, and unable to control one's behavior.

**aggression**: Angry or violent behavior, thoughts, or feelings.

**background check**: The process of looking up public records, especially any criminal history.

**mayhem:** Violence; disorder.

**safe havens:** Places of security and peace.

**social skills**: The abilities necessary to communicate and get along with others.

**universal violence prevention programs**: School-based programs offered to every child in a school or grade in order to teach about the problem of violence and how to prevent it.

**zero tolerance**: A practice or policy that imposes severe punishment, with no exceptions, for rule breaking.

# Bibliography

## Books

James Bow, *Gangs* (Straight Talk About…). New York: Crabtree, 2013.

Roman Espejo, ed., *Violent Video Games* (At Issue). Farmington Hills, MI: Greenhaven, 2014.

Kim Etingoff, *Gunman on Campus* (Safety First). Broomall, PA: Mason Crest, 2014.

Judy L. Hasday, *Forty-Nine Minutes of Madness* (Disasters: People in Peril). Berkeley Heights, NJ: Enslow, 2013.

Lori Hile, *Bullying* (Teen Issues). Hampshire, UK: Raintree, 2012.

Marilyn E. Smith, Matthew Monteverde, and Henrietta M. Lily, *School Violence and Conflict Resolution* (Teen Mental Health). New York: Rosen, 2012.

## Articles

"Should You Worry about School Violence?," TeensHealth, Kids Health.org, 2012. http://kidshealth.org/teen/school_jobs/bullying /school_violence.html#.

# Websites

**Bullying. No Way!** (http://bullyingnoway.gov.au/). This website from Australia has information and advice for students at different age levels about bullying and how to stop it.

**McGruff the Crime Dog** (www.mcgruff.org/). McGruff's website gives kids fun lessons on combating the crime of bullying.

**SAVE.org** (http://nationalsave.org/). SAVE stands for "Students Against Violence Everywhere." It is a national organization of youth chapters dedicated to preventing violent behavior. Students can learn about forming their own chapters or explore the information available on the website.

**School Violence: Weapons, Crime & Bullying** (www.nssc1.org/). This website has a section of articles with "Advice for Children and Teens."

**Stop Bullying.gov—Kids** (www.stopbullying.gov/kids/). This site from the US government explains what bullying is, how to prevent it, and how to respond when it happens.

**TeenHelp.com** (www.teenhelp.com/index.html). This website offers information and advice to teens and their parents on a variety of issues. Click the links to such topics as Teen Depression, Teen Violence, and Teen Stress to learn more.

# Index

# About the Author

**Toney Allman** holds degrees from Ohio State University and the University of Hawaii. She currently lives in Virginia, where she enjoys a rural lifestyle, as well as researching and writing about a variety of topics for students.